SKILLS FOR SUCCESS

with Windows® 7

GETTING STARTED

KRIS TOWNSEND

Prentice Hall

Boston Columbus Indianapolis New York San Francisco Upper Saddle River
Amsterdam Cape Town Dubai London Madrid Milan Munich Paris Montréal Toronto
Delhi Mexico City São Paulo Sydney Hong Kong Seoul Singapore Taipei Tokyo

Library of Congress Cataloging-in-Publication Data

Townsend, Kris.
  Skills for success with Windows 7: getting started / by Kris Townsend.
     p. cm.
  ISBN 0-13-511290-7
  1. Microsoft Windows (Computer file)   2. Operating systems (Computers)   I. Title.
QA76.76.O63T6965 2009
005.4'46—dc22   2009035257

Editor in Chief: *Michael Payne*
AVP/Executive Acquisitions Editor: *Stephanie Wall*
Product Development Manager: *Eileen Bien Calabro*
Editorial Project Manager: *Virginia Guariglia*
Development Editor: *Ginny Bess Munroe*
Editorial Assistant: *Nicole Sam*
AVP/Director of Online Programs, Media: *Richard Keaveny*
AVP/Director of Product Development, Media: *Lisa Strite*
Editor—Digital Learning & Assessment: *Paul Gentile*
Product Development Manager, Media: *Cathi Profitko*
Media Project Manager, Editorial: *Alana Coles*
Media Project Manager, Production: *John Cassar*
Director of Marketing: *Kate Valentine*
Senior Marketing Manager: *Tori Olsen Alves*
Marketing Coordinator: *Susan Osterlitz*

Marketing Assistant: *Darshika Vyas*
Senior Managing Editor: *Cynthia Zonneveld*
Associate Managing Editor: *Camille Trentacoste*
Production Project Manager: *Virginia Guariglia*
Senior Operations Supervisor: *Natacha Moore*
Senior Art Director: *Jonathan Boylan*
Art Director: *Anthony Gemmellaro*
Text and Cover Designer: *Anthony Gemmellaro*
Manager, Rights and Permissions: *Shannon Barbe*
Supplements Development Editor: *Tiffany Bottolfson*
Full-Service Project Management: *MPS Content Services, a Macmillan Company*
Composition: *MPS Content Services, a Macmillan Company*
Printer/Binder: *Courier/Kendallville*
Cover Printer: *Lehigh/Phoenix*
Typeface: *Minion 10.5/12.5*

Credits and acknowledgments borrowed from other sources and reproduced, with permission, in this textbook appear on appropriate page within text.

Microsoft® and Windows® are registered trademarks of the Microsoft Corporation in the U.S.A. and other countries. Screen shots and icons reprinted with permission from the Microsoft Corporation. This book is not sponsored or endorsed by or affiliated with the Microsoft Corporation.

Prentice Hall
is an imprint of

www.pearsonhighered.com

10 9 8 7 6 5 4 3 2 1
ISBN-10: 0-13-511290-7
ISBN-13: 978-0-13-511290-8

Table of Contents

Contributors

We thank the following people for their hard work and support in making Skills For Success all that it is!

Instructor Resource Authors

Ralph DeArazoza	*Miami Dade College*
Jeanette Dix	*Ivy Tech State College*
Dennis Faix	*Harrisburg Area Community College*
Tomeko Smith	*Kings College—Charlotte*
Paul Weaver	*Bossier Parish Community College*
Dawn Wood	*Technically Speaking Consultants*

Technical Editors

Janice Snyder
Joyce Nielsen
Janet Pickard

Reviewers

Laurel Aagard	*Sierra College*
John Alcorcha	*MTI College*
Barry Andrews	*Miami Dade College*
Natalie Andrews	*Sinclair Community College*
Wilma Andrews	*Virginia Commonwealth University School of Business*
Bridget Archer	*Oakton Community College*
Greg Ballinger	*Miami Dade College*
Terry Bass	*University of Massachusetts, Lowell*
Rocky Belcher	*Sinclair Community College*
Nannette Bibby	*Miami Dade College*
Alisa Brown	*Pulaski Technical College*
Eric Cameron	*Passaic Community College*
Trey Cherry	*Edgecombe Community College*
Kim Childs	*Bethany University*
Pauline Chohonis	*Miami Dade College*
Lennie Cooper	*Miami Dade College*
Gail Cope	*Sinclair Community College*
Chris Corbin	*Miami Dade College*
Tommi Crawford	*Miami Dade College*
Martin Cronlund	*Anne Arundel Community College*
Jennifer Day	*Sinclair Community College*
Ralph DeArazoza	*Miami Dade College*

Loorna DeDuluc	*Miami Dade College*
Caroline Delcourt	*Black Hawk College*
Michael Discello	*Pittsburgh Technical Institute*
Kevin Duggan	*Midlands Technical Community College*
Barbara Edington	*St. Francis College*
Donna Ehrhart	*Genesee Community College*
Tushnelda Fernandez	*Miami Dade College*
Arlene Flerchinger	*Chattanooga State Tech Community College*
Hedy Fossenkemper	*Paradise Valley Community College*
Kent Foster	*Winthrop University*
Arlene Franklin	*Bucks County Community College*
George Gabb	*Miami Dade College*
Deb Geoghan	*Bucks County Community College*
Jessica Gilmore	*Highline Community College*
Victor Giol	*Miami Dade College*
Linda Glassburn	*Cuyahoga Community College, West*
Deb Gross	*Ohio State University*
Rachelle Hall	*Glendale Community College*
Marie Hartlein	*Montgomery County Community College*
Diane Hartman	*Utah Valley State College*
Patrick Healy	*Northern Virginia Community College—Woodbridge*
Lindsay Henning	*Yavapai College*
Kermelle Hensley	*Columbus Technical College*
Mary Carole Hollingsworth	*GA Perimeter*
Stacey Gee Hollins	*St. Louis Community College—Meramec*
Joan Ivey	*Lanier Technical College*
Kay Johnston	*Columbia Basin College*
Sally Kaskocsak	*Sinclair Community College*
Hazel Kates	*Miami Dade College*
Charles Kellermann	*Northern Virginia Community College Woodbridge*
John Kidd	*Tarrant County Community College*
Chris Kinnard	*Miami Dade College*
Kelli Kleindorfer	*American Institute of Business*
Kurt Kominek	*Northeast State Technical Community College*
Dianne Kotokoff	*Lanier Technical College*
Jean Lacoste	*Virginia Tech*
Gene Laughrey	*Northern Oklahoma College*

David LeBron	*Miami Dade College*	Melissa Prinzing	*Sierra College*
Kaiyang Liang	*Miami Dade College*	Pat Rahmlow	*Montgomery County Community College*
Linda Lindaman	*Black Hawk College*	Kamaljeet Sanghera	*George Mason University*
Felix Lopez	*Miami Dade College*	Teresa Sept	*College of Southern Idaho*
Nicki Maines	*Mesa Community College*	Gary Sibbits	*St. Louis Community College-Meramec*
Cindy Manning	*Big Sandy Community and Technical College*	Janet Siert	*Ellsworth Community College*
Patri Mays	*Paradise Valley Community College*	Robert Sindt	*Johnson County Community College*
Sandy McCormack	*Monroe Community College*	Robert Smolenski	*Delaware County Community College*
Lee McKinley	*GA Perimeter*	Patricia Snyder	*Midlands Technical Community College*
Eric Meyer	*Miami Dade College*	Diane Stark	*Phoenix College*
Jackie Meyers	*Sinclair Community College*	Linda Stoudemayer	*Lamar Institute of Technology*
Kathryn Miller	*Big Sandy Community and Technical College, Pikeville Campus*	Linda Switzer	*Highline Community College*
Kathy Morris	*University of Alabama, Tuscaloosa*	Margaret Taylor	*College of Southern Nevada*
Linda Moulton	*Montgomery County Community College*	Martha Taylor	*Sinclair Community College*
Ryan Murphy	*Sinclair Community College*	Roseann Thomas	*Fayetteville Tech Community College*
Stephanie Murre Wolf	*Moraine Park Technical College*	Ingrid Thompson-Sellers	*GA Perimeter*
Jackie Myers	*Sinclair Community College*	Daniel Thomson	*Keiser University*
Dell Najera	*El Paso Community College, Valle Verde Campus*	Barb Tollinger	*Sinclair Community College*
Scott Nason	*Rowan Cabarrus Community College*	Cathy Urbanski	*Chandler Gilbert Community College*
Paula Neal	*Sinclair Community College*	Philip Vavalides	*Guilford Technical Community College*
Eloise Newsome	*Northern Virginia Community College— Woodbridge*	Pete Vetere	*Montgomery County Community College— West Campus*
Ellen Orr	*Seminole Community College*	Asteria Villegas	*Monroe College*
Carol Ottaway	*Chemeketa Community College*	Michael Walton	*Miami Dade College*
Denise Passero	*Fulton-Montgomery Community College*	Teri Weston	*Harford Community College*
Janet Pickard	*Chattanooga State Tech Community College*	Julie Wheeler	*Sinclair Community College*
Floyd Pittman	*Miami Dade College*	Debbie Wood	*Western Piedmont Community College*
		Thomas Yip	*Passaic Community College*
		Matt Zullo	*Wake Technical Community College*

A Microsoft® Office textbook that recognizes how students learn today–

Skills for Success
with Windows 7 *Getting Started*

- **10 x 8.5 Format –** Easy for students to read and type at the same time by simply propping the book up on the desk in front of their monitor

- **Clearly Outlined Skills –** Each skill is presented in a single two-page spread so that students can easily follow along

- **Numbered Steps and Bulleted Text –** Students don't read long paragraphs or text, but they will read information presented concisely

- **Easy-to-Find Student Data Files –** Visual key shows students how to locate and interact with their data files

Start Here – Students know exactly where to start and what their starting file will look like

Outcome – Shows students up front what their completed project will look like

Skills List – A visual snapshot of what skills they will complete in the chapter

Sequential Pagination – Saves you and your students time in locating topics and assignments

Skills for Success

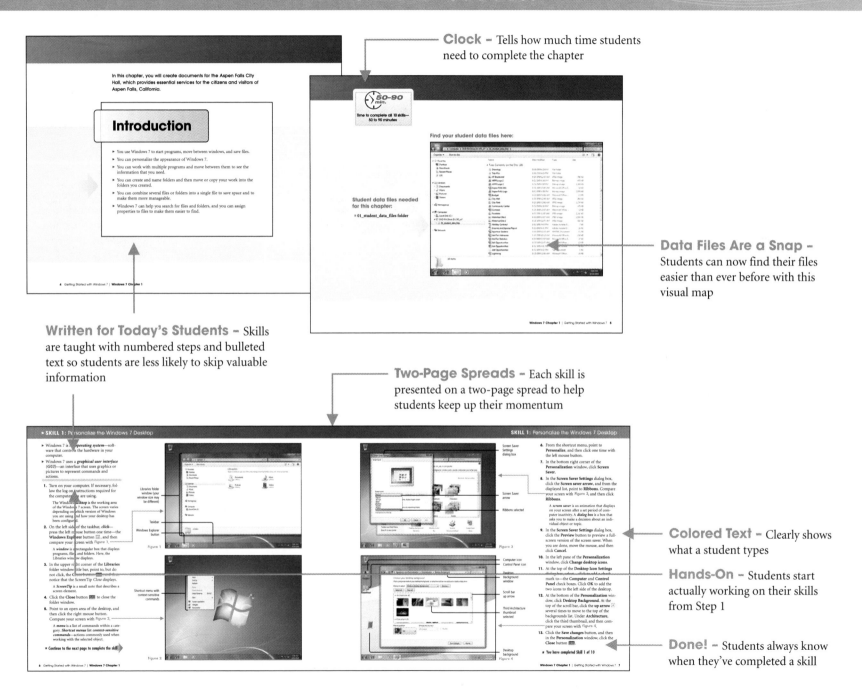

Clock – Tells how much time students need to complete the chapter

Data Files Are a Snap – Students can now find their files easier than ever before with this visual map

Written for Today's Students – Skills are taught with numbered steps and bulleted text so students are less likely to skip valuable information

Two-Page Spreads – Each skill is presented on a two-page spread to help students keep up their momentum

Colored Text – Clearly shows what a student types

Hands-On – Students start actually working on their skills from Step 1

Done! – Students always know when they've completed a skill

Skills for Success

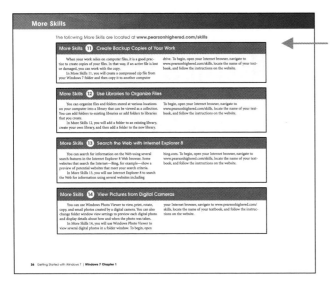

More Skills – Additional skills included online

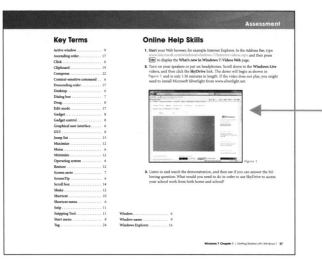

Online Project – Students practice using Microsoft Help online to help prepare them for using the applications on their own

End-of-Chapter Material – Several levels of assessment so you can assign the material that best fits your students' needs

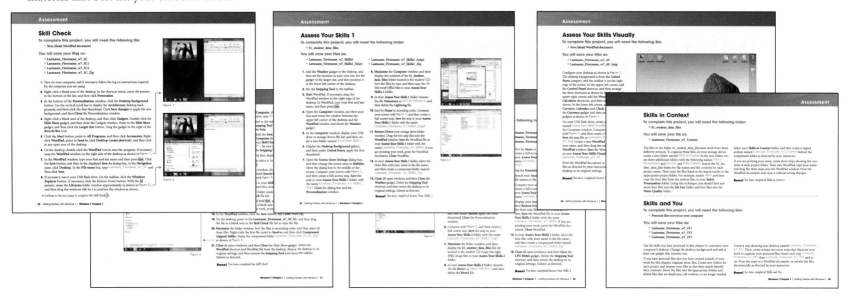

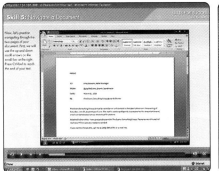   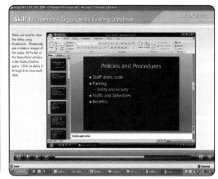

Videos! – Each skill within a chapter comes with a video that includes audio, which demonstrates the skill

Instructor Materials

All Videos and Instructor materials available on the IRCD

Instructor's Manual – Teaching tips and additional resources for each chapter

Assignment Sheets – Lists all the assignments for the chapter, you just add in the course information, due dates and points. Providing these to students ensures they will know what is due and when

Scripted Lectures – Classroom lectures prepared for you

Annotated Solution Files – Coupled with the scoring rubrics, these create a grading and scoring system that makes grading so much easier for you

Power Point Lectures – PowerPoint presentations for each chapter

Prepared Exams – Exams for each chapter and for each application

Scoring Rubrics – Can be used either by students to check their work or by you as a quick check-off for the items that need to be corrected

Syllabus Templates – for 8-week, 12-week, and 16-week courses

Test Bank – Includes a variety of test questions for each chapter

Companion Website – Online content such as the More Skills Projects, Online Study Guide, Glossary, and Student Data Files are all at www.pearsonhighered.com/skills

About the Author

Kris Townsend is an Information Systems instructor at Spokane Falls Community College in Spokane, Washington. Kris earned bachelor's degrees in Education and Business, and a master's degree in Education. He has also worked as a public school teacher and as a systems analyst. Kris can often be found outdoors exploring and photographing historic routes of Lewis and Clark and the Nez Perce.

This book is dedicated to the students at Spokane Falls Community College. Their adventures guide the way.

—KRIS TOWNSEND

CHAPTER **1**

Getting Started with Windows 7

► You use Windows 7 to work with your computer. For example, you start programs, move between windows, and save your work.

► In Windows 7, you organize your work by naming files and placing those files into folders that you create.

Your starting screen will look like this:

SKILLS

At the end of this chapter, you will be able to:

Skill 1   Personalize the Windows 7 Desktop

Skill 2   Add and Remove Gadgets

Skill 3   Add Shortcuts

Skill 4   Move Between Windows and Customize the Taskbar

Skill 5   Resize, Move, and Scroll Windows

Skill 6   Use Windows Explorer and Create Folders

Skill 7   Move and Rename Folders and Copy Files

Skill 8   Move, Rename, and Delete Files

Skill 9   Compress Files and Use the Address Bar

Skill 10   Describe and Find Files and Folders

MORE SKILLS

More Skills 11 Create Backup Copies of Your Work

More Skills 12 Use Libraries to Organize Files

More Skills 13 Search the Web with Internet Explorer 8

More Skills 14 View Pictures from Digital Cameras

Outcome

Using the skills listed to the left will enable you to configure your computer similar to these:

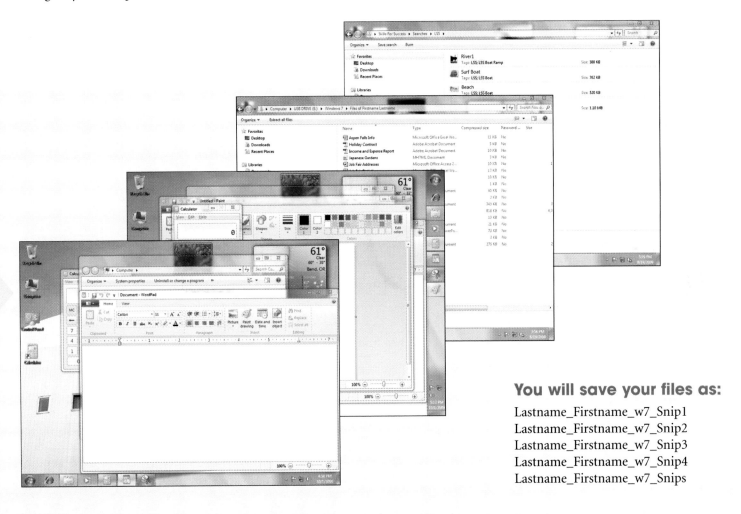

You will save your files as:

Lastname_Firstname_w7_Snip1
Lastname_Firstname_w7_Snip2
Lastname_Firstname_w7_Snip3
Lastname_Firstname_w7_Snip4
Lastname_Firstname_w7_Snips

In this chapter, you will create documents for the Aspen Falls City Hall, which provides essential services for the citizens and visitors of Aspen Falls, California.

Introduction

- ▶ You use Windows 7 to start programs, move between windows, and save files.

- ▶ You can personalize the appearance of Windows 7.

- ▶ You can work with multiple programs and move between them to see the information that you need.

- ▶ You can create and name folders and then move or copy your work into the folders you created.

- ▶ You can combine several files or folders into a single file to save space and to make them more manageable.

- ▶ Windows 7 can help you search for files and folders, and you can assign properties to files to make them easier to find.

Time to complete all 10 skills—50 to 90 minutes

Find your student data files here:

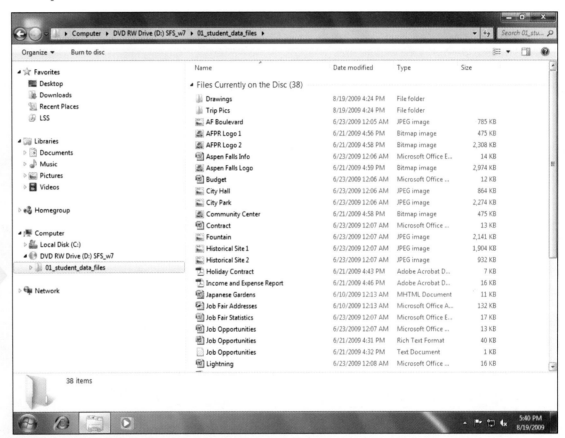

Student data files needed for this chapter:

- 01_student_data_files folder

► Windows 7 is an *operating system*—software that controls the hardware in your computer.

► Windows 7 uses a *graphical user interface (GUI)*—an interface that uses graphics or pictures to represent commands and actions.

1. Turn on your computer. If necessary, follow the log on instructions required for the computer you are using.

   The Windows *desktop* is the working area of the Windows 7 screen. The screen varies depending on which version of Windows you are using and how your desktop has been configured.

2. On the left side of the taskbar, *click*— press the left mouse button one time—the **Windows Explorer** button 📁, and then compare your screen with Figure 1.

   A *window* is a rectangular box that displays programs, files, and folders. Here, the Libraries window displays.

3. In the upper right corner of the **Libraries** folder window title bar, point to, but do not click, the **Close** button 🗙, and then notice that the ScreenTip *Close* displays.

   A *ScreenTip* is a small note that describes a screen element.

4. Click the **Close** button 🗙 to close the folder window.

5. Point to an open area of the desktop, and then click the right mouse button. Compare your screen with Figure 2.

   A *menu* is a list of commands within a category. *Shortcut menus* list *context-sensitive commands*—actions commonly used when working with the selected object.

■ **Continue to the next page to complete the skill**

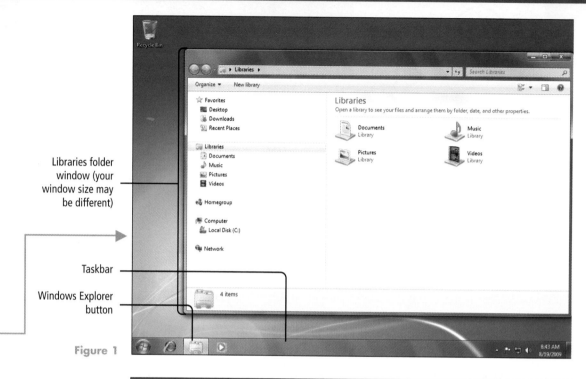

Libraries folder window (your window size may be different)

Taskbar

Windows Explorer button

Figure 1

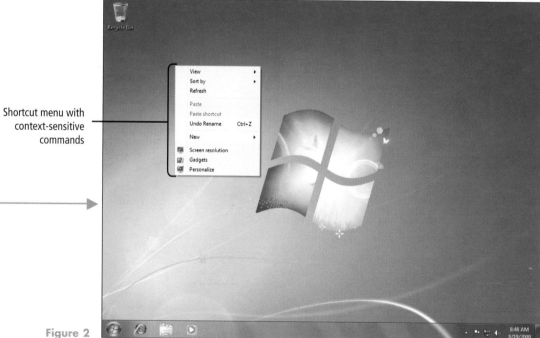

Shortcut menu with context-sensitive commands

Figure 2

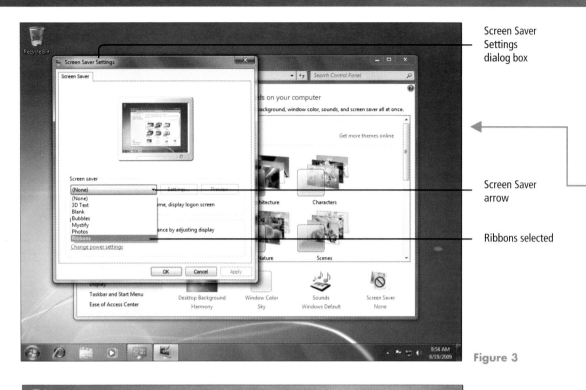

Screen Saver
Settings
dialog box

Screen Saver
arrow

Ribbons selected

Figure 3

Computer icon
Control Panel icon

Desktop
Background
window

Scroll bar
up arrow

Third Architecture
thumbnail
selected

Desktop
background

Figure 4

6. From the shortcut menu, point to **Personalize**, and then click one time with the left mouse button.

7. In the bottom right corner of the **Personalization** window, click **Screen Saver**.

8. In the **Screen Saver Settings** dialog box, click the **Screen saver arrow**, and from the displayed list, point to **Ribbons**. Compare your screen with **Figure 3**, and then click **Ribbons**.

> A *screen saver* is an animation that displays on your screen after a set period of computer inactivity. A *dialog box* is a box that asks you to make a decision about an individual object or topic.

9. In the **Screen Saver Settings** dialog box, click the **Preview** button to preview a full-screen version of the screen saver. When you are done, move the mouse, and then click **Cancel**.

10. In the left pane of the **Personalization** window, click **Change desktop icons**.

11. At the top of the **Desktop Icon Settings** dialog box, select—click to add a check mark to—the **Computer** and **Control Panel** check boxes. Click **OK** to add the two icons to the left side of the desktop.

12. At the bottom of the **Personalization** window, click **Desktop Background**. At the top of the scroll bar, click the **up arrow** ▲ several times to move to the top of the backgrounds list. Under **Architecture**, click the third thumbnail, and then compare your screen with **Figure 4**.

13. Click the **Save changes** button, and then in the **Personalization** window, click the **Close** button ▣.

■ **You have completed Skill 1 of 10**

▶ *Gadgets* are dynamic programs that can be moved anywhere on your screen.

▶ The *Start menu* gives you access to all of the programs on your computer.

1. In an open area of the desktop, right-click to display a shortcut menu. From the shortcut menu, click **Gadgets**. Compare your screen with **Figure 1**.

2. In the **Gadgets** gallery, double-click the **Weather** gadget. In the **Gadgets** window, click the **Close** button ⊠.

3. Point to the **Weather** gadget to display the *gadget control*—a four-button tool set used to modify gadgets. In the gadget control, click the **Larger size** button ▣.

4. Click the gadget control **Options** button ▣, and then in the **Select current location** box, type Bend, OR

5. Press [Enter], and then click **OK** to display the current weather for Bend, Oregon.

6. Right-click the desktop, and then click **Gadgets**. In the **Gadgets** gallery, double-click the **Slide Show** gadget. Double-click to add a second **Slide Show** gadget, and then **Close** ⊠ the Gadgets window.

7. Point to the lower **Slide Show** gadget, and then in the gadget controls, click the **Close** button ⊠ to remove the gadget from the desktop.

8. On the remaining **Slide Show** gadget, point to the **Drag gadget** button ▦, and then *drag*—move the mouse while holding down the left mouse button and then release at the appropriate time—the gadget near the upper edge of the desktop as shown in **Figure 2**.

▪ **Continue to the next page to complete the skill**

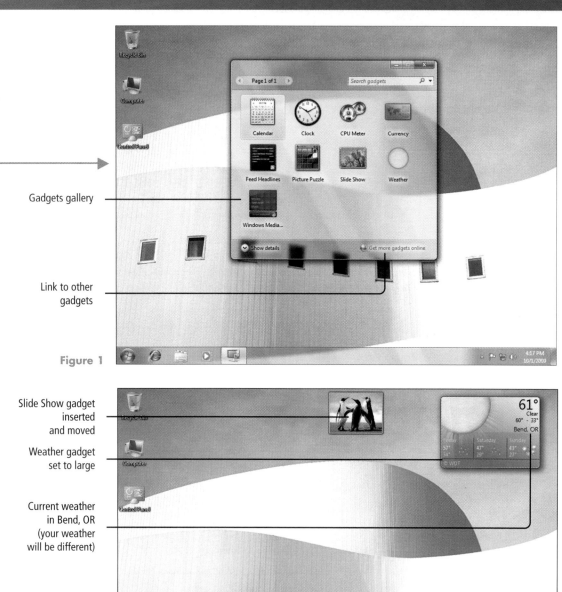

Gadgets gallery

Link to other gadgets

Figure 1

Slide Show gadget inserted and moved

Weather gadget set to large

Current weather in Bend, OR (your weather will be different)

Figure 2

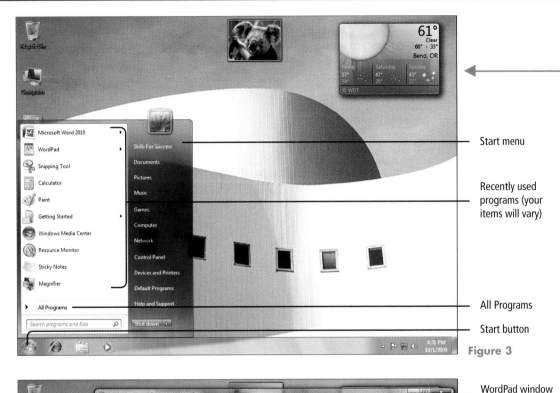

Start menu

Recently used
programs (your
items will vary)

All Programs

Start button

Figure 3

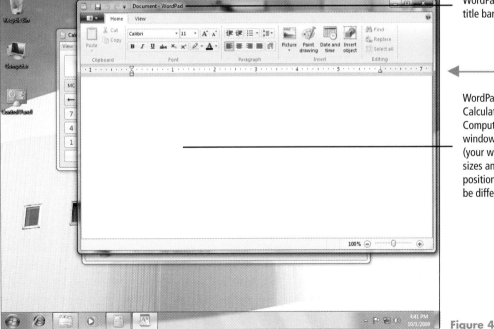

WordPad window
title bar

WordPad covers
Calculator and
Computer
windows
(your window
sizes and
positions may
be different)

Figure 4

9. In the lower left corner of the screen, point to and then click the **Start** button 🔘, and then compare your screen with Figure 3.

   The Start menu displays shortcuts to recently used program and common folder windows. The All Programs menu displays the programs installed on your computer.

   Your Start menu will display differently than the one in the figure. For example, your list of recently used programs will be different.

10. From the **Start** menu, point to, but do not click, **All Programs** to display a list of programs and program folders. Click the **Accessories** folder, and then from the list, click **Calculator**.

   The Calculator program opens, and the Start menu closes. The program's *window name*—*Calculator*—displays in the title bar.

11. Click the **Start** button 🔘 again. Near the middle of the right side of the **Start** menu, click **Computer**. If the Computer window covers the entire screen, in the upper right corner of the window, click the Restore Down button 🔲.

12. Click the **Start** button 🔘. In the **Search programs and files** box, type wordpad and then press Enter. If the WordPad window fills the entire screen, click the Restore Down button 🔲. Compare your screen with Figure 4.

   Windows often overlap, but the *active window*—the window in which typing or clicking occurs—displays on top of the other open windows. Here, WordPad is the active window.

   ■ **You have completed Skill 2 of 10**

▶ To make a frequently used program quickly available, you can pin a *shortcut*—an icon linked to another file or program that opens the file or program—to the Start menu or taskbar. You can also add shortcuts to the desktop.

1. Point to the **WordPad** window title bar. Click and then drag down and to the right to position the window below the **Computer** window title bar. On the left edge of the screen, be sure the three desktop icons display.

2. Click the **Start** button 🔘, point to **All Programs**, click **Accessories**, and then right-click **Calculator**.

3. From the displayed shortcut menu, click **Pin to Start Menu**. At the bottom of the **Start** menu, click the **Back** button, and notice that *Calculator* has been added to the pinned programs area as shown in Figure 1.

4. Click the **Start** button 🔘, point to **All Programs**, click **Accessories**, right-click **Calculator**, and then point to—but do not click—**Send to**. Notice the available commands on the *Send to* list, as shown in Figure 2.

5. From the shortcut menu, click **Desktop (create shortcut)**, and then click in any open area of the desktop to close the Start menu.

■ **Continue to the next page to complete the skill** ▶

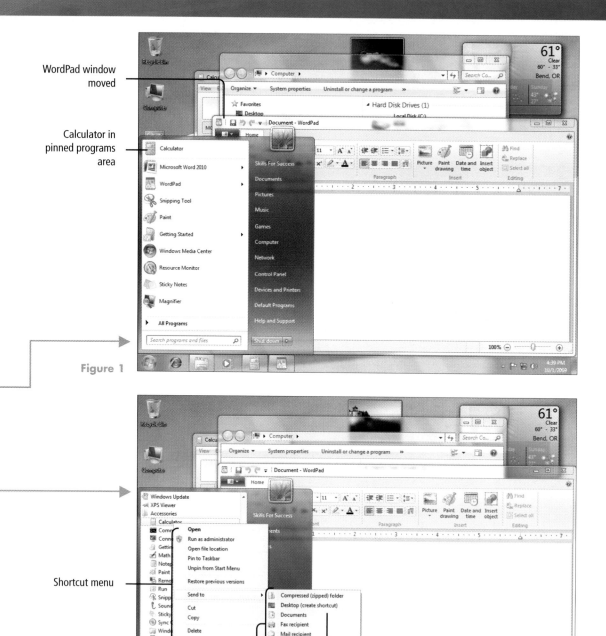

WordPad window moved

Calculator in pinned programs area

Figure 1

Shortcut menu

Send to submenu

Desktop (create shortcut) command

Figure 2

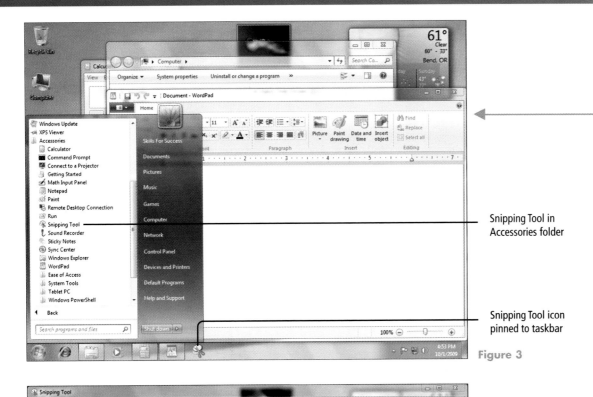

Snipping Tool in
Accessories folder

Snipping Tool icon
pinned to taskbar

Figure 3

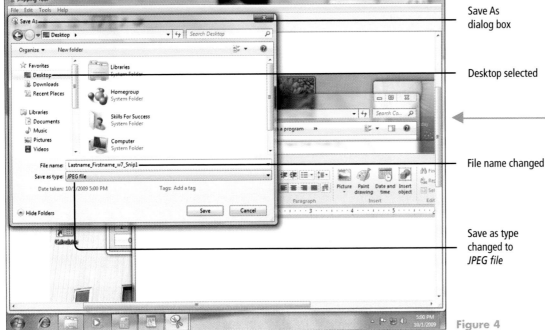

Save As
dialog box

Desktop selected

File name changed

Save as type
changed to
JPEG file

Figure 4

6. Click the **Start** button, point to **All Programs**, and then click **Accessories**. In the list of **Accessories** programs, right-click **Snipping Tool**, and then click **Pin to Taskbar**. Compare your screen with Figure 3.

   You can use *Snipping Tool* to capture a screen shot, or *snip*, of the entire screen or any object on your screen, and then annotate, save, or share the image. You will use this tool throughout this chapter.

7. Click the **WordPad** window to make it the active window. On the taskbar, click the **Snipping Tool** button.

8. In the **Snipping Tool** window, click the **arrow** to the right of the **New** button—the **New button arrow**—to display a list of snip types. From the list, click **Full-screen Snip**.

9. Near the top of the **Snipping Tool** window, click the **Save Snip** button. In the **Save As** dialog box, under **Favorites**, click **Desktop**. In the **File name** box, using your own last and first name, replace the file name—*Capture*—with Lastname_Firstname_w7_Snip1 Between words, use the underscore character—hold down Shift and then to the right of the 0, press -.

10. Click the **Save as type** box, and then from the menu, click **JPEG file**. Compare your screen with Figure 4, and then click **Save** to save the snip on the desktop.

11. In the upper right corner of the **Snipping Tool** window, click the **Close** button. Notice that your file displays as an icon on the desktop.

■ **You have completed Skill 3 of 10**

▶ You can *maximize* a window, which enlarges the window to occupy the entire screen, and you can *restore* a window, which reduces the window to the size it was before being maximized.

▶ You can also *minimize* a window, which reduces the window to a button on the taskbar, removing it from the desktop without actually closing it.

1. In the **WordPad** window, click the **Maximize** button so that the window covers the entire screen as shown in **Figure 1**.

2. Click the **Restore Down** button to return the window to its former shape, size, and location.

3. In the **WordPad** window, click the **Minimize** button.

4. In the taskbar, click the **Calculator** button to restore the **Calculator** window. Then, click the **WordPad** button to restore the **WordPad** window.

5. Move the pointer to the lower right corner of the taskbar to point to the **Show desktop** button as shown in **Figure 2**.

6. Click the **Show desktop** button to hide all windows. Click the **Show desktop** button again to display all open windows.

7. In the taskbar, click the **Calculator** button to make the Calculator the active window.

8. Point to the **Calculator** title bar, hold down the left mouse button, and then *shake*—move the window back and forth quickly—the window to close all other windows.

■ Continue to the next page to complete the skill ▶

WordPad maximized

Maximize button changes to Restore Down button

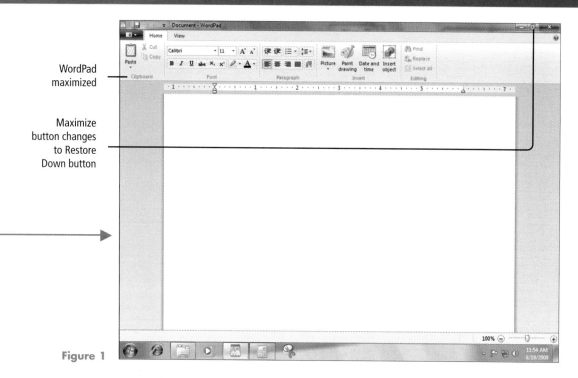

Figure 1

Transparent windows (only if Aero feature is enabled)

Show desktop button

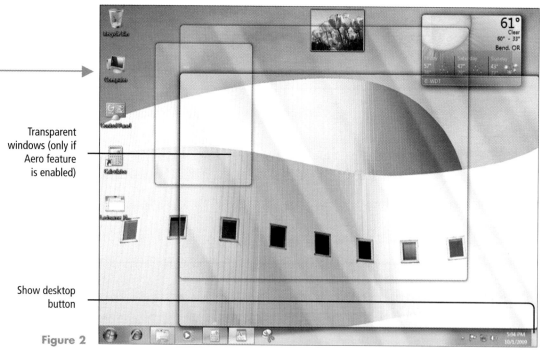

Figure 2

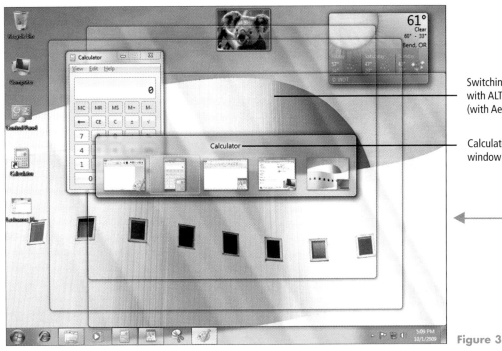

Switching windows
with ALT + TAB
(with Aero enabled)

Calculator is active
window

Figure 3

9. Shake the **Calculator** window again to display all open windows.

10. Click the **Start** button 🟦, point to **All Programs**, click **Accessories**, and then click **Paint**. If the Paint window is maximized, click the Restore Down button 🔲.

11. Hold down the [Alt] key, and then press the [Tab] key. Continue to hold down [Alt], and press [Tab] several times. Notice that the selected window moves from left to right in the list of thumbnails. Move to the **Calculator** window as shown in **Figure 3**, and then release [Alt].

12. On the taskbar, point to the **Computer** icon and right-click to display a *jump list*—a list of related files or commands that you might want to jump to.

13. Right-click an open area of the taskbar, and then from the shortcut menu, click **Properties**. In the **Taskbar and Start Menu Properties** dialog box, click the **Taskbar location on screen arrow**, and then click **Right**. Click **OK** and compare your screen with **Figure 4**.

14. In the taskbar, click the **Snipping Tool** button ✂. In the **Snipping Tool** window, click the **New button arrow**, and then click **Full-screen Snip**. Click the **Save Snip** button 💾, and then in the **Save As** dialog box, click **Desktop**. In the **File name** box, type Lastname_Firstname_w7_Snip2 With **JPEG file** selected, click **Save**, and then **Close** 🞫 the Snipping Tool.

15. Use the technique you practiced to return the taskbar to the bottom of the desktop.

   ■ **You have completed Skill 4 of 10**

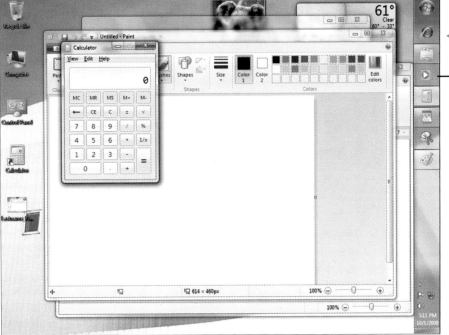

Taskbar displays
on right side of
screen

Figure 4

▶ You can move, resize, and scroll windows to view the information you need.

1. On the right side of the taskbar, click the **Show desktop** button ▌ to hide all of the windows.

2. On the taskbar, click the **Windows Explorer** button. Move the pointer to the lower right corner of the **Computer** window to display the ◨ pointer as shown in **Figure 1**.

3. Drag diagonally up and to the left until you see scroll bars, and then release the mouse button. Adjust as necessary so that the **Computer** window is the approximate size of the one shown in **Figure 2**.

> A *scroll bar* is added to the window whenever the window contains more content than it can display. Here, two scroll bars display. In a scroll bar, the *scroll box* provides a visual indication of your location in the window. The size of the scroll box varies to indicate the relative size of the information.

4. In the **Computer** window **Navigation** pane, at the bottom of the vertical scroll bar, click the **down arrow** ▼ two times to scroll down.

5. On the same scroll bar, click the **up arrow** ▲ and hold down the left mouse button to scroll to the top.

6. Point to the scroll box, and then drag it downward.

7. At the top of the **Computer** window, point to a blank area in the title bar. Drag the window to the top edge of the desktop, and then release the mouse button to maximize the window.

■ **Continue to the next page to complete the skill** ➤

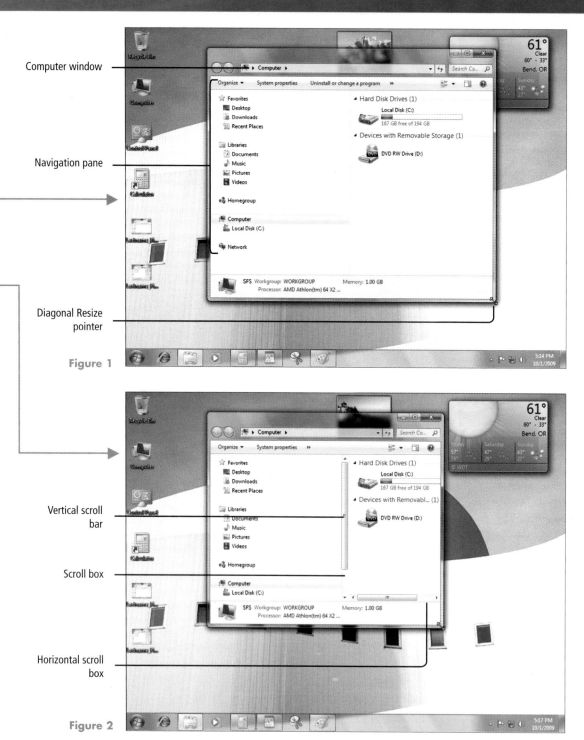

Computer window

Navigation pane

Diagonal Resize pointer

Figure 1

Vertical scroll bar

Scroll box

Horizontal scroll box

Figure 2

WordPad window
snapped to edge
of desktop

Figure 3

8. Drag the title bar down to restore the window to its original size, but not its original location.

9. In the **Computer** window, click the **Close** button ⊠. In the taskbar, right-click the **Paint** button ⧉, and then click **Close window**. Use the same technique to close the **Calculator** window.

10. In the taskbar, click the **WordPad** button to make it the active window. Drag the WordPad window title bar to the right edge of the desktop to snap the WordPad window as shown in **Figure 3**.

11. In the **WordPad** window, type your first and last name, and then press ⏎. On the desktop, click the **Lastname_Firstname_ w7_Snip1** icon to display its full name. Drag the icon to the line below your name in the WordPad document, and then release the mouse button.

> A copy of the snip is inserted into the WordPad document.

12. Drag the **Lastname_Firstname_w7_Snip2** file to the line below the figure you previously inserted into the WordPad document. Scroll to the top of the **WordPad** window, and then compare your screen with **Figure 4**.

13. In the top, left corner of the **WordPad** title bar, click the **Save** button 🖫. In the **Save As** dialog box, in the **Navigation** pane, click **Desktop**. In the **File name** box, type Lastname_Firstname_w7_Snips and then click **Save**.

14. **Close** ⊠ the WordPad window.

■ **You have completed Skill 5 of 10**

Your own name

Snip1 inserted

Snip2 inserted

Figure 4

► **Windows Explorer** is a program used to create and manage folders, and to copy, move, sort, and delete files.

► When you have a new category of files to store, you can create a new folder.

1. On the taskbar, click the **Windows Explorer** button 📁.

2. If the window is not maximized, drag the title bar to the top of the screen. Alternately, on the right side of the title bar, click the Maximize button ⬜.

3. On the toolbar, click the **Organize** button, and then point to **Layout**. If Details pane is not checked, click to select it.

4. In the **Navigation** pane on the left side of the **Computer** window, click **Computer**. Compare your screen with **Figure 1**. If necessary, to the left of Computer, click the open arrow ▷.

    The open arrow changes to a filled arrow pointing downward ◢.

5. Insert your USB flash drive or another removable drive. If the AutoPlay dialog box displays, click Close ✖. In the Navigation pane, under Computer, click your removable drive. Compare your screen with **Figure 2**.

    For this chapter, the file list is empty; your storage device or drive may already contain files and folders and may be named differently.

■ **Continue to the next page to complete the skill**

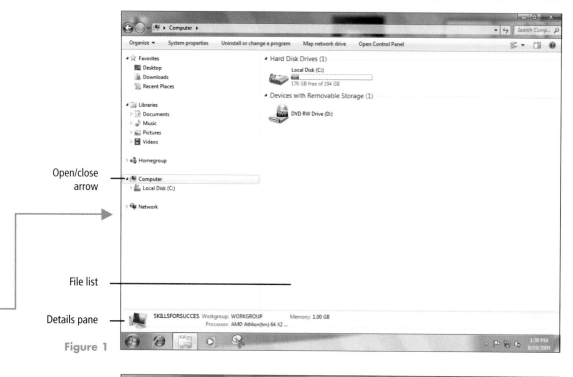

Open/close arrow

File list

Details pane

Figure 1

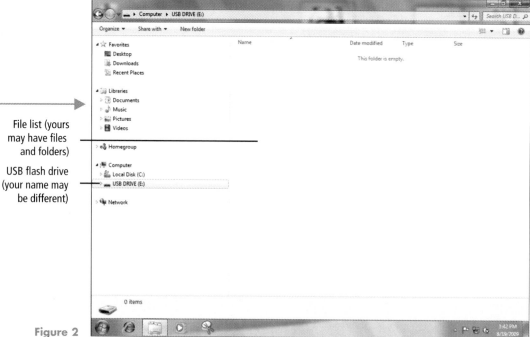

File list (yours may have files and folders)

USB flash drive (your name may be different)

Figure 2

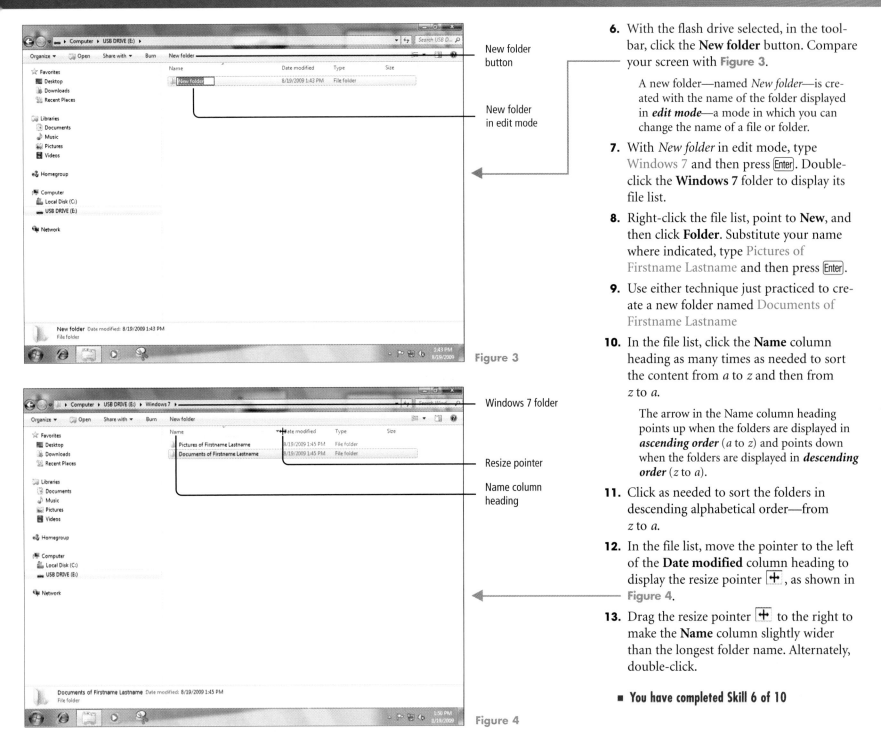

New folder
button

New folder
in edit mode

Figure 3

Windows 7 folder

Resize pointer

Name column
heading

Figure 4

6. With the flash drive selected, in the tool-bar, click the **New folder** button. Compare your screen with **Figure 3**.

> A new folder—named *New folder*—is created with the name of the folder displayed in *edit mode*—a mode in which you can change the name of a file or folder.

7. With *New folder* in edit mode, type Windows 7 and then press Enter. Double-click the **Windows 7** folder to display its file list.

8. Right-click the file list, point to **New**, and then click **Folder**. Substitute your name where indicated, type Pictures of Firstname Lastname and then press Enter.

9. Use either technique just practiced to create a new folder named Documents of Firstname Lastname

10. In the file list, click the **Name** column heading as many times as needed to sort the content from *a* to *z* and then from *z* to *a*.

> The arrow in the Name column heading points up when the folders are displayed in *ascending order* (*a* to *z*) and points down when the folders are displayed in *descending order* (*z* to *a*).

11. Click as needed to sort the folders in descending alphabetical order—from *z* to *a*.

12. In the file list, move the pointer to the left of the **Date modified** column heading to display the resize pointer ✛, as shown in **Figure 4**.

13. Drag the resize pointer ✛ to the right to make the **Name** column slightly wider than the longest folder name. Alternately, double-click.

■ **You have completed Skill 6 of 10**

▶ You can move the folders, including the files in the folders, from another location to your flash drive or other storage device.

1. Navigate to the location where your student files for this book are stored. They may be stored on a CD, in a course management system, on a hard drive, or on a shared network drive. In this chapter, the data CD is used.

2. In the **Navigation** pane, click the **CD open arrow** ▷, and then click the **01_student_data_files** folder.

3. In the **Navigation** pane, if necessary, click the **open arrow** ▷ to the left of your storage device as shown in **Figure 1**.

4. Near the top of the file list, drag the **Drawings** folder to the **Navigation** pane directly on top of your **Windows 7** folder. When the ScreenTip says *Copy to Windows 7*, release the mouse button.

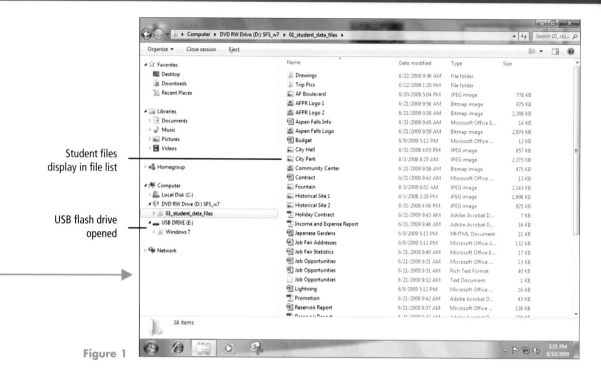

Student files display in file list

USB flash drive opened

Figure 1

5. Repeat the procedure just practiced to copy the **Trip Pics** folder to your **Windows 7** folder.

6. In the **Navigation** pane, click your **Windows 7** folder. In the file list, right-click the **Drawings** folder, click **Rename**, type Drawings of Firstname Lastname and then press Enter. Compare your screen with **Figure 2**.

7. In the **Navigation** pane, under **Computer**, locate and click the folder named **01_student_data_files** to display its file list.

8. Near the middle of the file list, drag the **City Hall** file to your **Windows 7** folder.

■ **Continue to the next page to complete the skill**

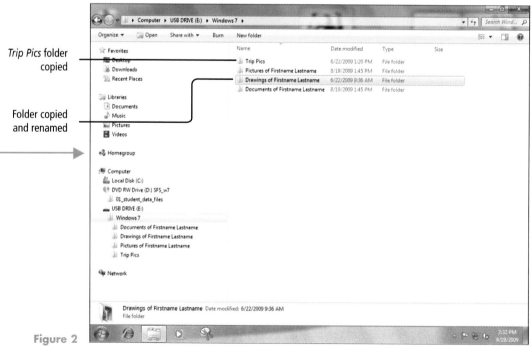

Trip Pics folder copied

Folder copied and renamed

Figure 2

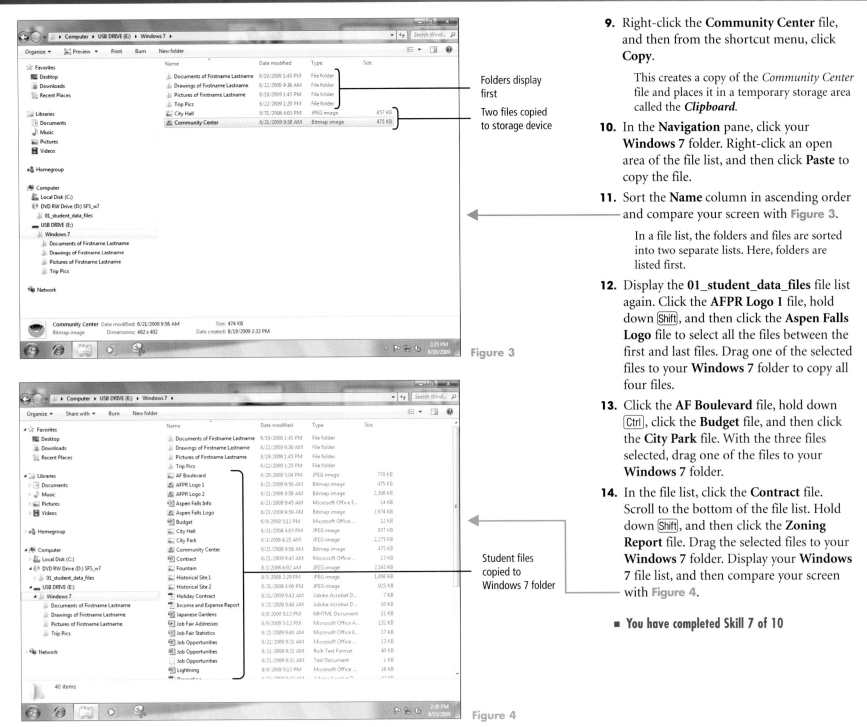

Folders display first

Two files copied to storage device

Figure 3

Student files copied to Windows 7 folder

Figure 4

9. Right-click the **Community Center** file, and then from the shortcut menu, click **Copy**.

This creates a copy of the *Community Center* file and places it in a temporary storage area called the *Clipboard*.

10. In the **Navigation** pane, click your **Windows 7** folder. Right-click an open area of the file list, and then click **Paste** to copy the file.

11. Sort the **Name** column in ascending order and compare your screen with **Figure 3**.

In a file list, the folders and files are sorted into two separate lists. Here, folders are listed first.

12. Display the **01_student_data_files** file list again. Click the **AFPR Logo 1** file, hold down Shift, and then click the **Aspen Falls Logo** file to select all the files between the first and last files. Drag one of the selected files to your **Windows 7** folder to copy all four files.

13. Click the **AF Boulevard** file, hold down Ctrl, click the **Budget** file, and then click the **City Park** file. With the three files selected, drag one of the files to your **Windows 7** folder.

14. In the file list, click the **Contract** file. Scroll to the bottom of the file list. Hold down Shift, and then click the **Zoning Report** file. Drag the selected files to your **Windows 7** folder. Display your **Windows 7** file list, and then compare your screen with **Figure 4**.

■ **You have completed Skill 7 of 10**

► When you drag a file or folder to another place on the same drive, the file or folder is moved—not copied—to that location.

► You can rename or delete files when you no longer need them.

1. If necessary, display your **Windows 7** file list.

2. In the file list, click the **Type** column header to sort the files by file type. Point to the right border of the **Type** column heading, and then with the ⊞ pointer, double-click to resize the column.

3. In the file list, use the wheel in the middle of your mouse or the vertical scroll bar to scroll down until you can see all of the **Microsoft Office Word Document** files. If necessary, in the Navigation pane, click your Windows 7 folder open arrow ▷ to display its folders, and scroll as needed to display all four folders as shown in **Figure 1**.

4. Click the **Budget** file, hold down Shift, and then click the **Survey Letter** file to select all the Word documents. Drag the selected files to the **Documents of Firstname Lastname** folder to move them to the folder.

5. In the **Navigation** pane, click the **Documents of Firstname Lastname** folder to display the moved files as shown in **Figure 2**.

Sorted by file type

Word document files

Windows 7 folders

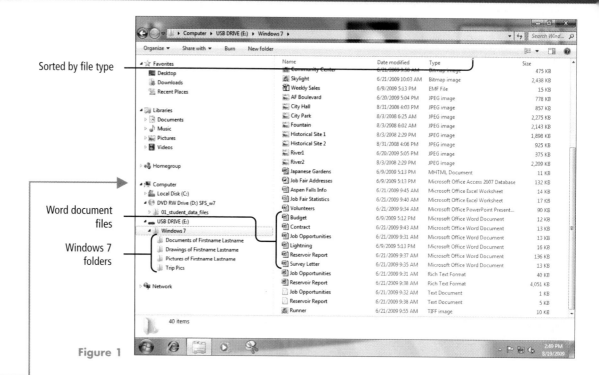

Figure 1

Word documents moved to folder

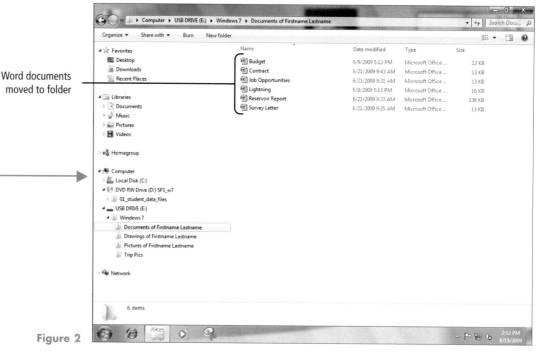

Figure 2

■ **Continue to the next page to complete the skill** ▷

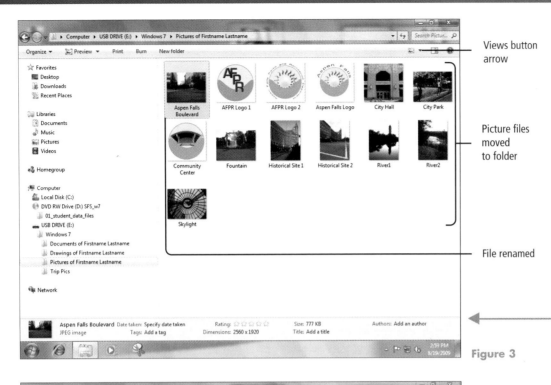

Views button arrow

Picture files moved to folder

File renamed

Figure 3

6. In the **Navigation** pane, click your **Windows 7** folder. Use the technique just practiced to move the eight **JPEG image** files to the **Pictures of Firstname Lastname** folder.

7. Move the five Bitmap images—**BMP File**—to the **Pictures of Firstname Lastname** folder.

8. In the **Navigation** pane, click the **Pictures of Firstname Lastname** folder. On the toolbar, click the **Views button arrow** [icon], and then if it is not already selected, click **Large Icons**.

9. In the file list, right-click the **AF Boulevard** file, and then click **Rename**. Type Aspen Falls Boulevard and then press Enter. Compare your screen with Figure 3.

10. In the file list, right-click the **Historical Site 2** file, and then click **Delete**. The **Delete File** message box displays, as shown in Figure 4.

   When you delete files from removable storage such as a USB flash drive, the files are typically deleted permanently.

11. In the **Delete File** message box, click **Yes**.

12. In the upper left corner of the window, click the **Back** button [icon] to move back to your Windows 7 folder. Alternately, in the Navigation pane, click your Windows 7 folder.

13. In the file list, right-click the **Trip Pics** folder, and then click **Delete**. In the displayed **Delete Folder** message box, click **Yes**.

   When you delete a folder, all files in the folder are also deleted.

■ **You have completed Skill 8 of 10**

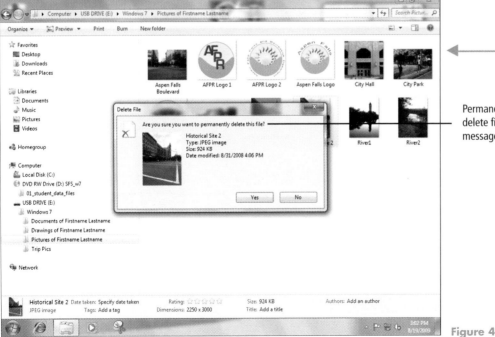

Permanently delete file message

Figure 4

► You can *compress*—reduce the file size of—one or more files into a single file. Compression is often used to combine many files into one file for easy distribution.

► You can use the address bar at the top of the Windows Explorer window to move to a desired location.

1. With your **Windows 7** file list displayed, sort the **Name** column in ascending order.

2. Click the **Aspen Falls Info** file, hold down Shift, and then click the **Zoning Report** file. If necessary, in the Details pane, click Show more details, and then notice that the 17 files have a total size of about 5 MB as shown in **Figure 1**. ────────

3. In the file list, right-click one of the selected files, and then from the displayed shortcut menu, point to **Send to**. Click **Compressed (zipped) folder**, and then wait a moment for the files to be compressed.

   The compressed folder displays the name of the file that you right-clicked, and it is in edit mode so you can change the file name.

4. With the compressed file in edit mode, type Files of Firstname Lastname and then press Enter. Sort by file name and click **Files of Firstname Lastname** to display its details as shown in **Figure 2**. ────────

   The compressed folder is about 1.6 MB—which is about 68% smaller than the original file.

■ **Continue to the next page to complete the skill**

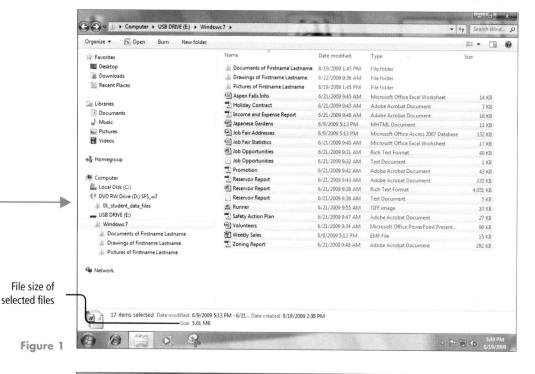

File size of
selected files

Figure 1

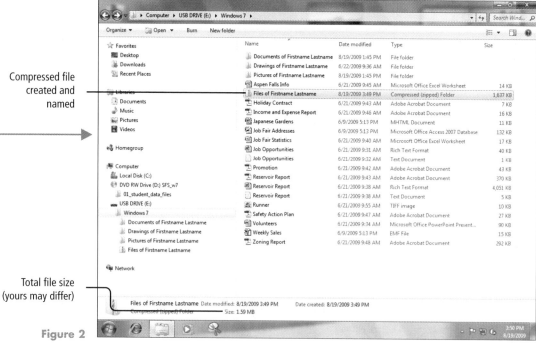

Compressed file
created and
named

Total file size
(yours may differ)

Figure 2

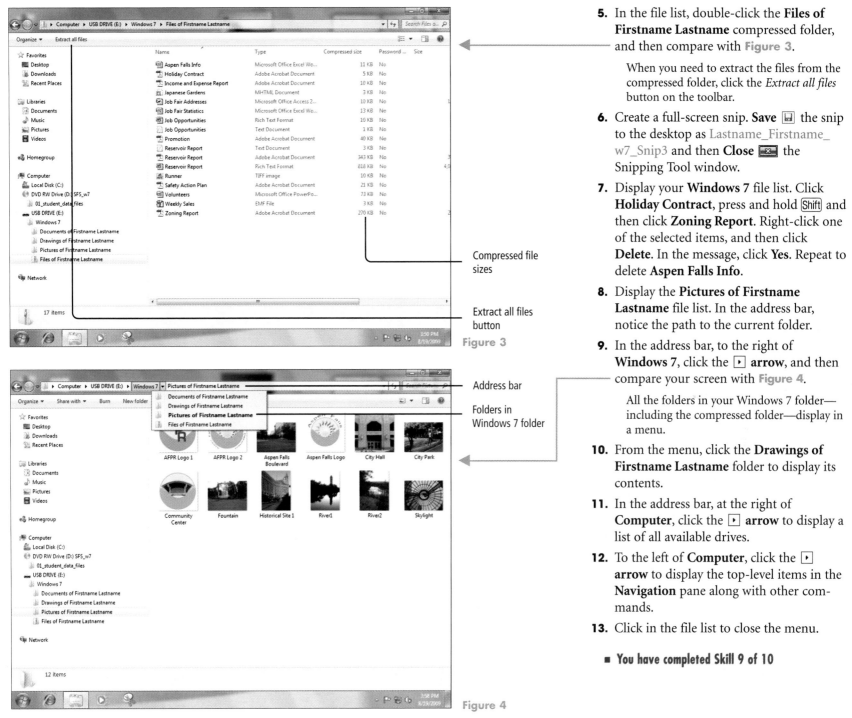

Compressed file sizes

Extract all files button

Figure 3

Address bar

Folders in Windows 7 folder

Figure 4

5. In the file list, double-click the **Files of Firstname Lastname** compressed folder, and then compare with **Figure 3**.

   When you need to extract the files from the compressed folder, click the *Extract all files* button on the toolbar.

6. Create a full-screen snip. **Save** 🖫 the snip to the desktop as Lastname_Firstname_w7_Snip3 and then **Close** ☒ the Snipping Tool window.

7. Display your **Windows 7** file list. Click **Holiday Contract**, press and hold [Shift] and then click **Zoning Report**. Right-click one of the selected items, and then click **Delete**. In the message, click **Yes**. Repeat to delete **Aspen Falls Info**.

8. Display the **Pictures of Firstname Lastname** file list. In the address bar, notice the path to the current folder.

9. In the address bar, to the right of **Windows 7**, click the ⏵ **arrow**, and then compare your screen with **Figure 4**.

   All the folders in your Windows 7 folder—including the compressed folder—display in a menu.

10. From the menu, click the **Drawings of Firstname Lastname** folder to display its contents.

11. In the address bar, at the right of **Computer**, click the ⏵ **arrow** to display a list of all available drives.

12. To the left of **Computer**, click the ⏵ **arrow** to display the top-level items in the **Navigation** pane along with other commands.

13. Click in the file list to close the menu.

   ■ **You have completed Skill 9 of 10**

► Windows 7 has several search methods you can use to find files and folders.

► You can also add *tags*—custom file properties that help you find and organize your files.

1. From your storage device, display the **Drawings of Firstname Lastname** file list, and then click the first file—**Beach**.

2. Move the pointer to the line at the top of the **Details** pane to display the ⚓ pointer, and then drag to display three lines of details.

3. In the **Details** pane, in the **Tags** box, click the text **Add a tag**. Type LSS and then press ➡. Type LSS Boat and then compare your screen with **Figure 1**. ————

4. Press Enter to confirm the tags. Use the procedure just practiced—type, do not use the check boxes—to add the same two tags to the **Surf Boat** file.

5. In the **Navigation** pane, click the **Pictures of Firstname Lastname** folder, and then click the file **River1**. Type the following tags: LSS and LSS Boat Ramp and then press Enter.

6. In the **Details** pane, click the **Title** box, type River Station and then press Enter.

7. In the file list, right-click the **River1** file, and then click **Properties**. In the **Properties** dialog box, click the **Details** tab.

8. Under **Description**, click the fourth **Rating** star from the left. Under **Origin**, click the **Copyright** box, and then type Public Domain Compare your screen with **Figure 2**, and then click **OK**. ————

■ Continue to the next page to complete the skill ▶

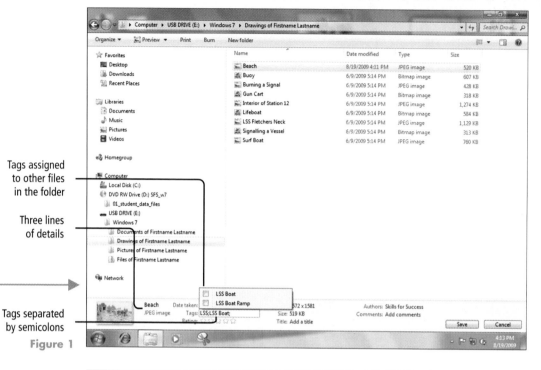

Tags assigned to other files in the folder

Three lines of details

Tags separated by semicolons

Figure 1

Properties dialog box Details tab

Description properties

Copyright property

Figure 2

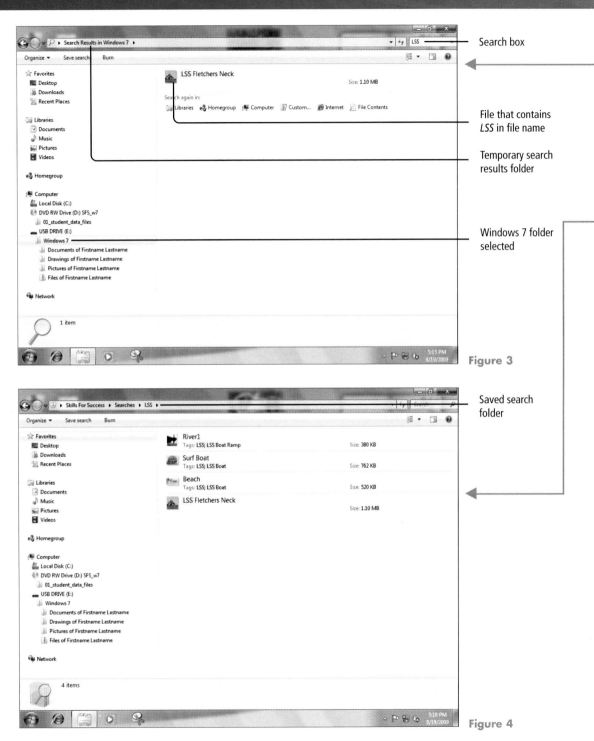

Figure 3

Figure 4

Search box

File that contains *LSS* in file name

Temporary search results folder

Windows 7 folder selected

Saved search folder

9. Display your **Windows 7** file list. Click in the search box, type LSS and compare your screen with **Figure 3**.

10. In the file list below the displayed file, notice the search alternatives that are available. Under **Search again in**, click **File Contents** to display four files.

11. On the toolbar, click the **Save search** button, and then click **Save**. At the top of the **Navigation** pane, click **Favorites**. In the file list, double-click **LSS** to open the saved search as shown in **Figure 4**.

12. Create a full-screen snip. Click the **Save Snip** button 🔲. In the **Save As** dialog box, scroll down and click to display your **Windows 7** file list. On the toolbar, click the **New folder** button. Type Snips and then press Enter two times. In the **File name** box, type Lastname_Firstname_ w7_Snip4 Click **Save**, and then click **Close** ▣.

13. Use the skills practiced in this chapter to copy the three snips and WordPad document located on the desktop to the **Snips** folder.

14. In your **Snips** folder, open the WordPad document. Scroll to the bottom of the document, and then drag the **Snip3** and **Snip4** files into the document. If you are directed to print this project, press Ctrl + P, and then click Print. Click **Save** 🔲, and then **Close** ▣ WordPad.

15. **Close** ▣ the **Computer** window. **Delete** the files and shortcuts you saved on the desktop, and then **Close** ▣ the gadgets that you added.

Done! You have completed Skill 10 of 10 and your document is complete!

More Skills

The following More Skills are located at **www.pearsonhighered.com/skills**

More Skills Create Backup Copies of Your Work

When your work relies on computer files, it is a good practice to create copies of your files. In that way, if an active file is lost or damaged, you can work with the copy.

In More Skills 11, you will create a compressed zip file from your Windows 7 folder and then copy it to another computer drive. To begin, open your Internet browser, navigate to www.pearsonhighered.com/skills, locate the name of your textbook, and follow the instructions on the website.

More Skills Use Libraries to Organize Files

You can organize files and folders stored at various locations on your computer into a library that can be viewed as a collection. You can add folders to existing libraries or add folders to libraries that you create.

In More Skills 12, you will add a folder to an existing library, create your own library, and then add a folder to the new library.

To begin, open your Internet browser, navigate to www.pearsonhighered.com/skills, locate the name of your textbook, and follow the instructions on the website.

More Skills Search the Web with Internet Explorer 8

You can search for information on the Web using several search features in the Internet Explorer 8 Web browser. Some websites that search the Internet—Bing, for example—show a preview of potential websites that meet your search criteria.

In More Skills 13, you will use Internet Explorer 8 to search the Web for information using several websites including bing.com. To begin, open your Internet browser, navigate to www.pearsonhighered.com/skills, locate the name of your textbook, and follow the instructions on the website.

More Skills View Pictures from Digital Cameras

You can use Windows Photo Viewer to view, print, rotate, copy, and email photos created by a digital camera. You can also change folder window view settings to preview each digital photo and display details about how and when the photo was taken.

In More Skills 14, you will use Windows Photo Viewer to view several digital photos in a folder window. To begin, open your Internet browser, navigate to www.pearsonhighered.com/skills, locate the name of your textbook, and follow the instructions on the website.

Key Terms

Online Help Skills

1. Start your Web browser, for example Internet Explorer. In the Address Bar, type www.microsoft.com/windows/windows-7/features/videos.aspx and then press Enter to display the **What's new in Windows 7: Videos Web** page.

2. Turn on your speakers or put on headphones. Scroll down to the **Windows Live** videos, and then click the **SkyDrive** link. The demo will begin as shown in Figure 1 and is only 1:36 minutes in length. If the video does not play, you might need to install Microsoft Silverlight from www.silverlight.net.

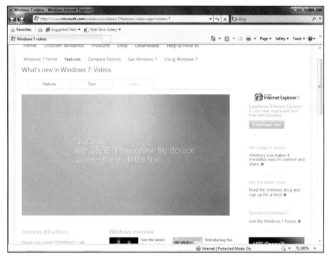

Figure 1

3. Listen to and watch the demonstration, and then see if you can answer the following question: What would you need to do in order to use SkyDrive to access your school work from both home and school?

Matching

Match each term in the second column with its correct definition in the first column by writing the letter of the term on the blank line in front of the correct definition.

____ **1.** Software that controls the hardware attached to your computer.

____ **2.** An interface that uses graphics or pictures to represent commands and actions.

____ **3.** The working area of the Windows 7 screen.

____ **4.** A graphic representation—often a small image on a button—that enables you to run a program or a program function.

____ **5.** A small note, usually displayed in a yellow box, which provides information about or describes a screen element.

____ **6.** A dynamic program that can be moved anywhere on your screen.

____ **7.** A program that captures a screen or part of a screen.

____ **8.** To remove the window from the screen without closing it.

____ **9.** To increase the size of a window to fill the screen.

____ **10.** A program that enables you to create and manage folders, and to copy, move, sort, and delete files.

A Desktop

B Gadget

C Graphical User Interface

D Icon

E Maximize

F Minimize

G Operating System

H ScreenTip

I Snipping Tool

J Windows Explorer

Multiple Choice

Choose the correct answer.

1. GUI is an acronym for _____.
   A. General universal information
   B. Globally unique identifier
   C. Graphical user interface

2. You can activate a shortcut menu by placing the pointer over an object and clicking the _____ mouse button.
   A. Left
   B. Middle
   C. Right

3. A box that asks you to make a decision about an individual object or topic is called a _____ box.
   A. Dialog
   B. Question
   C. Text

4. The button on the left side of the taskbar that is used to open programs, change system settings, find Windows help, or shut down the computer is called the _____ button.
   A. Go
   B. Start
   C. Windows

5. The files and folders stored in the selected disk drive or folder are displayed in the _____ list.
   A. Content
   B. File
   C. Navigation

6. When you create a new folder, the folder name displays in _____ mode.
   A. Copy
   B. Delete
   C. Edit

7. When you copy an item, it is stored in the _____, a temporary storage area in Windows.
   A. Bit locker
   B. CGI bin
   C. Clipboard

8. You can _____ a file or files to reduce the size of the files or combine files to make them easier to send.
   A. Compress
   B. Copy
   C. Merge

9. When you create a search folder, the search name displays in the Navigation pane in the _____ category.
   A. Favorites
   B. Found
   C. Recent Searches

10. A custom file property that is read during searches is the _____ property.
    A. Locate
    B. Statistics
    C. Tags

Topics for Discussion

1. Recall that you can create folders when you have new categories of files to store. Consider what files you currently have and will have on your computer or storage device. What folders do you need to organize these files, and what names would you assign to each folder?

2. Recall that you can pin shortcuts to commonly used programs to the Start menu and taskbar. What programs do you think you would pin to the Start menu or taskbar?

Skill Check

To complete this project, you will need the following file:

- New, blank WordPad document

You will save your files as:

- Lastname_Firstname_w7_SC
- Lastname_Firstname_w7_SC1
- Lastname_Firstname_w7_SC2
- Lastname_Firstname_w7_SC_Zip

1. Turn on your computer, and if necessary, follow the log on instructions required for the computer you are using.

2. Right-click a blank area of the desktop. In the shortcut menu, move the pointer to the bottom of the list, and then click **Personalize**.

3. At the bottom of the **Personalization** window, click the **Desktop Background** button. Use the vertical scroll bar to display the **Architecture** desktop backgrounds, and then click the first thumbnail. Click **Save changes** to apply the new background, and then **Close** the Personalization window.

4. Right-click a blank area of the desktop, and then click **Gadgets**. Double-click the **Slide Show** gadget, and then **Close** the Gadgets window. Point to the **Slide Show** gadget, and then click the **Larger size** button. Drag the gadget to the right of the **Recycle Bin** icon.

5. Click the **Start** button, point to **All Programs**, and then click **Accessories**. Right-click **WordPad**, point to **Send to**, click **Desktop (create shortcut)**, and then click in any open area of the desktop.

6. On the desktop, double-click the **WordPad** icon to start the program. If necessary, snap the **WordPad** window on the right side of the desktop as shown in **Figure 1**.

7. In the **WordPad** window, type your first and last name and then press (Enter). Click the **Save** button, and then in the displayed **Save As** dialog box, in the **Navigation** pane, click **Desktop**. In the **File name** box, type Lastname_Firstname_w7_SC and then click **Save**.

8. If necessary, insert your USB flash drive. On the taskbar, click the **Windows Explorer** button. If necessary, click the Restore Down button. With the 🔍 pointer, resize the **Libraries** folder window approximately as shown in **Figure 2**, and then drag the window's title bar to position the window as shown.

■ Continue to the next page to complete this Skill Check ▶

Figure 1

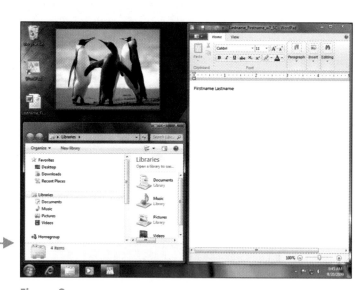

Figure 2

9. In the **Navigation** pane, under **Computer**, display the contents of your storage device. Click the **New folder** button, type Skill Check and then press Enter.

10. If necessary, pin the Snipping Tool to the taskbar. On the taskbar, click the **Snipping Tool** button. In the **Snipping Tool** window, click the **New button arrow**, and then click **Full-screen Snip**.

11. In the **Snipping Tool** window, click the **Save Snip** button. In the **Save As** dialog box, scroll down to display the **Computer** drives. Click your flash drive **arrow** to display its folders, and display your **Skill Check** file list. In the **File name** box, type Lastname_Firstname_w7_SC1 Be sure the **Save as type** box displays **JPEG file**, click **Save**, and then close the **Snipping Tool** window.

12. **Maximize** the folder window, and then display the **Skill Check** file list.

13. Click the snip—**JPEG image**—file to select it. In the **Details** pane, click the **Tags** box, type desktop and then press Enter.

14. In the upper right corner of the window, click in the search box, type desktop and then press Enter. In the displayed **Search Results** folder, click **File Contents** and then compare your screen with **Figure 3**.

Figure 3

15. Create a full-screen snip, **Save** it in your **Skill Check** folder as Lastname_Firstname_w7_SC2 and then close the Snipping Tool window.

16. In the upper right corner of the folder window, click the **Restore Down** button, and then display your **Skill Check** file list.

17. Click the first snip file, press and hold Shift, and then click the second snip file. Drag one of the selected files to a blank area below your name in the **WordPad** window. If you are printing your work, print the WordPad document.

18. In the **WordPad** window, click the **Save** button, and **Close** WordPad.

19. On the desktop, point to the **Lastname_Firstname_w7_SC** file, and then drag the file to a blank area in the **Skill Check** file list to copy the file.

20. **Maximize** the folder window. Sort the files in ascending order, and then select all three files. Right-click the first file, point to **Send to**, and then click **Compressed (zipped) folder**. Name the compressed folder Lastname_Firstname_w7_SC_Zip as shown in **Figure 4**.

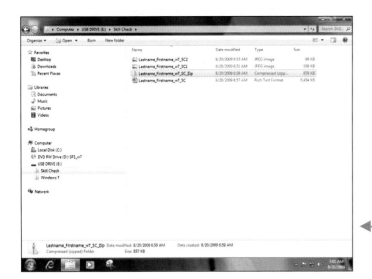

Figure 4

21. **Close** all open windows, and then **Close** the Slide Show gadget. Delete the **WordPad** shortcut and WordPad file from the desktop. Return the desktop to its original settings, and then remove the **Snipping Tool** icon from the taskbar. Submit as directed.

Done! You have completed the Skill Check

Assess Your Skills 1

To complete this project, you will need the following folder:

- 01_student_data_files

You will save your files as:

- Lastname_Firstname_w7_Skills1
- Lastname_Firstname_w7_Skills1_Snip1
- Lastname_Firstname_w7_Skills1_Snip2
- Lastname_Firstname_w7_Skills1_Zip

1. Add the **Weather** gadget to the desktop, and then set the location to your own city. Set the gadget to the larger size, and then position it in the lower left corner of the desktop.

2. Pin the **Snipping Tool** to the taskbar.

3. **Start** WordPad. If necessary, snap the WordPad window to the right edge of the desktop. In WordPad, type your first and last name, and then press Enter.

4. Open the **Computer** window, and then position and resize the window between the upper left corner of the desktop and the **WordPad** window and above the **Weather** gadget.

5. In the **Computer** window, display your USB drive or storage device file list, and then create a new folder named Assess Your Skills 1

6. Display the **Desktop Background** gallery, and then under **United States**, apply the first thumbnail.

7. Open the **Screen Saver Settings** dialog box, and then change the screen saver to **Bubbles**. Move the dialog box to the middle of the screen. Compare your screen with **Figure 1**, and then create a full-screen snip. **Save** the snip in your **Assess Your Skills 1** folder with the name Lastname_Firstname_w7_Skills1_ Snip1 **Close** the dialog box and the **Personalization** window.

8. **Maximize** the **Computer** window, and then display the contents of the **01_student_data_files** folder located in the student CD. Sort the files by type, and then copy the 10 *Microsoft Office* files to your **Assess Your Skills 1** folder.

9. In your **Assess Your Skills 1** folder, rename the file **Volunteers** as Job Fair Volunteers and then delete the **Lightning** file.

10. Sort by **Name** in ascending order. Compare your screen with **Figure 1**, and then create a full-screen snip. **Save** the snip in your **Assess Your Skills 1** folder with the name Lastname_Firstname_w7_Skills1_Snip2

11. **Restore Down** your storage drive folder window. Drag the two snip files into the **WordPad** window. **Save** the WordPad file in your **Assess Your Skills 1** folder with the name Lastname_Firstname_w7_Skills1 If you are printing your work, print the WordPad document. **Close** WordPad.

12. In your **Assess Your Skills 1** folder, select the three files with your name in the file name, and then create a compressed folder named Lastname_Firstname_ w7_Skills1_Zip

13. **Close** all open windows, and then **Close** the **Weather** gadget. Delete the **Snipping Tool** shortcut, and then return the desktop to its original settings. Submit as directed.

Done! You have completed Assess Your Skills 1

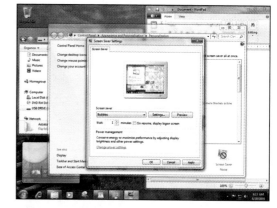

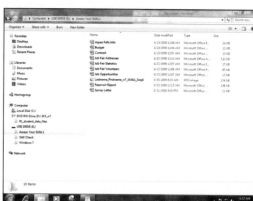

Figure 1

Assess Your Skills 2

To complete this project, you will need the following folder:

- 01_student_data_files

You will save your files as:

- Lastname_Firstname_w7_Skills2
- Lastname_Firstname_w7_Skills2_Snip1
- Lastname_Firstname_w7_Skills2_Snip2
- Lastname_Firstname_w7_Skills2_Snip3
- Lastname_Firstname_w7_Skills2_Zip

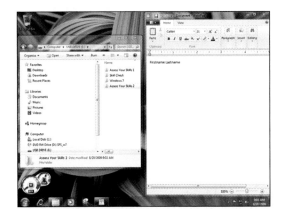

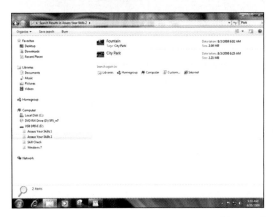

Figure 1

1. Add the **CPU Meter** gadget to the desktop and position it in the lower left corner of the desktop. Pin the **Snipping Tool** to the taskbar.

2. **Start** WordPad. If necessary, snap the **WordPad** window to the right edge of the desktop. In WordPad, type your first and last name, and then press [Enter].

3. **Open** the **Computer** folder window, and then position and resize the window between the left edge of the screen and the **WordPad** window and above the **CPU Meter** gadget.

4. In the **Computer** window, display your USB drive or storage device file list, and then create a new folder named Assess Your Skills 2

5. Display the **Desktop Background** gallery, and then under **Nature**, apply the third thumbnail. **Close** the Personalization window.

6. Compare with **Figure 1**, and then create a full-screen snip. **Save** the snip in your **Assess Your Skills 2** folder with the name Lastname_Firstname_w7_Skills2_Snip1

7. **Maximize** the folder window, and then display the **01_student_data_files** file list located in the student CD. Copy the eight *JPEG image* files to your **Assess Your Skills 2** folder.

8. In your **Assess Your Skills 2** folder, rename the file **River1** as Aspen Falls River and then delete the **River2** file.

9. Sort by **Name** in ascending order, and then create a full-screen snip. **Save** the snip in your **Assess Your Skills 2** folder with the name Lastname_Firstname_w7_Skills2_Snip2

10. Tag the **Fountain** file with the text City Park

11. Search your **Assess Your Skills 2** folder for file names or file contents with the text Park

12. Compare your screen with **Figure 1** and then create a full-screen snip. **Save** the snip in your **Assess Your Skills 2** folder with the name Lastname_Firstname_w7_Skills2_Snip3

13. Display your **Assess Your Skills 2** file list and then **Restore Down** the folder window. Drag the three snip files into the **WordPad** window. **Save** the WordPad file in your **Assess Your Skills 2** folder with the name Lastname_Firstname_w7_Skills2 If you are printing your work, print the WordPad document. **Close** WordPad.

14. In your **Assess Your Skills 2** folder, select the four files with your name in the file name, and then create a compressed folder named Lastname_Firstname_w7_Skills2_Zip

15. **Close** all open windows, and then **Close** the **CPU Meter** gadget. Delete the **Snipping Tool** shortcut, and then return the desktop to its original settings. Submit as directed.

Done! You have completed Assess Your Skills 2

Assess Your Skills Visually

To complete this project, you will need the following file:

- New, blank WordPad document

You will save your files as:

- Lastname_Firstname_w7_AV
- Lastname_Firstname_w7_AV_Snip

Configure your desktop as shown in **Figure 1**. The desktop background is from the **United States** category, and the taskbar is on the right edge of the screen. In the upper left corner, add the **Control Panel** shortcut, and then arrange the three shortcuts as shown in the figure. In the upper right corner, add the **WordPad**, **Paint**, and **Calculator** shortcuts, and then arrange them as shown. In the lower left corner, add the **Currency**, **Calendar**, and **Clock** gadgets. Enlarge the **Currency** gadget and then arrange the three gadgets as shown in **Figure 1**.

On your USB flash drive, create a new folder named Assess Your Skills Visually and then close the Computer window. Compare your desktop with **Figure 1**, and then create a full-screen snip. **Save** the snip file as Lastname_Firstname_w7_AV_Snip Create a new **WordPad** document, add your name, and then drag the snip file into the **WordPad** window. **Save** the WordPad document in your **Assess Your Skills Visually** folder as Lastname_Firstname_w7_AV

Print the WordPad document or submit your files as directed by your instructor. Return the desktop to its original settings.

Done! You have completed Assess Your Skills Visually

Figure 1

Skills in Context

To complete this project, you will need the following folder:

- **01_student_data_files**

You will save your file as:

- **Lastname_Firstname_w7_Context**

The files in the folder *01_student_data_files* have work from three different projects. To organize these files, on your storage device, create a new folder named Skills in Context In the new folder, create three additional folders with the following names: Safety Presentation and Job Fair and Water Quality Search the *01_student_data_files* folder for file names and file contents for each project name. Then copy the files listed in the search results to the appropriate project folder. For example, search safety and then copy the four files from the student files to your **Safety Presentation** folder. Using this technique, you should find and move four files into the **Job Fair** folder and four files into the **Water Quality** folder.

Select your **Skills in Context** folder, and then create a zipped archive named Lastname_Firstname_w7_Context Submit the compressed folder as directed by your instructor.

If you are printing your work, create three snips showing the contents of each project folder. Then start WordPad, type your name, and drag the three snips into the WordPad window. Print the WordPad document, and close it without saving changes.

Done! You have completed Skills in Context

Skills and You

To complete this project, you will need the following files:

- **Personal files stored on your computer**

You will save your files as:

- **Lastname_Firstname_w7_SY1**
- **Lastname_Firstname_w7_SY2**
- **Lastname_Firstname_w7_SY3**

Use the skills you have practiced in this chapter to customize your computer's desktop. Change the desktop background and add at least one gadget that interests you.

If you have personal files that you have created outside of your work for this chapter, organize those files. Create new folders for each project and rename your files so that they clearly identify their contents. Move the files into the appropriate folders and delete files that are duplicates, old versions, or no longer needed.

Create a snip showing your desktop named Lastname_Firstname_w7_SY1 Then, create at least two more snips that illustrate your work to organize your personal files. Name each snip Lastname_Firstname_w7_SY2 then Lastname_Firstname_w7_SY3 and so on. Print the snips in a WordPad document, or submit the files electronically as directed by your instructor.

Done! You have completed Skills and You

Glossary

Accelerator A feature that searches for specialized information using the text you select on a Web page.

Active window The window in which typing or clicking occurs.

Ascending order A sort order beginning with lower values and ending with higher values. For example, *a* to *z*.

AutoComplete A feature that stores the information and passwords that you enter into website forms so that you can automatically fill in other forms.

Backup A duplicate copy of computer files that can be used if the active copy is lost or damaged.

Click The action of pressing the left mouse button one time.

Clipboard A temporary storage area from which you can paste an item.

Compress To reduce the file size of one or more files into a single file that uses a *.zip* file extension.

Context-sensitive command An action commonly used when working with the selected object.

Descending order A sort order beginning with higher values and ending with lower values. For example, *z* to *a*.

Desktop The work area of the Windows 7 screen.

Dialog box A box that asks you to make a decision about an individual object or topic.

Drag To move the mouse while holding down the left mouse button and then releasing the button at the appropriate time.

Edit mode A mode in which you can change the name of a file or folder.

Gadget A dynamic program that can be moved anywhere on your screen.

Gadget control A four-button tool set used to modify gadgets.

Graphical user interface An interface that uses graphics or pictures to represent commands and actions.

GUI An acronym for graphical user interface.

Hyperlink Text or a picture that moves you to a new location or Web page when it is clicked.

InPrivate A feature that prevents Internet Explorer from collecting information as you browse.

Jump list A list of related files or commands that you might jump to.

Library A collection of files and folders stored at different locations on your computer that can be viewed as a single folder.

Maximize To enlarge a window to occupy the entire screen.

Menu A list of commands within a category.

Minimize To reduce a window to a button on the taskbar, removing it from the desktop without actually closing it.

Operating system Software that controls the hardware in your computer.

Pixel The smallest dot of color in a picture, screen, or printout.

Restore To reduce a window to the size it was before being maximized.

Screen saver An animation that displays on your screen after a set period of computer inactivity.

ScreenTip A small note that describes a screen element.

Scroll bar A screen element added to the window whenever the window contains more content than it can display.

Scroll box A box in the scroll bar that provides a visual indication of your location within a window.

Search provider A website designed specifically for searching the World Wide Web.

Shake To move a window back and forth quickly to open or close all other windows.

Shortcut An icon linked to another file or program that opens the file or program.

Shortcut menu A list of context-sensitive commands commonly used when working with the selected object.

Snip A screen shot captured using the Snipping Tool.

Snipping Tool A program that captures a screen or part of a screen.

Start menu A menu that gives you access to all the programs on your computer.

Tag A custom file property that helps you find and organize your files.

URL An address of a specific page on the Internet.

Web browser A program used to display Web pages and navigate the World Wide Web.

Window A rectangular box that displays programs, files, and folders.

Window name The name of a window that displays in the title bar.

Windows Explorer A program used to create and manage folders, and to copy, move, sort, and delete files.

Index

 The internet icon represents Index entries found within More Skills
on the Companion Website: www.pearsonhighered.com/skills